RECYCLED ART

Emily Kington

Contents

Paper Roll Crafts!

Ready to have fun... **10**

Spooky Mates **12**

Zoo Animals **16**

Hungry Frog **22**

Crafty Caterpillar **24**

Castle **28**

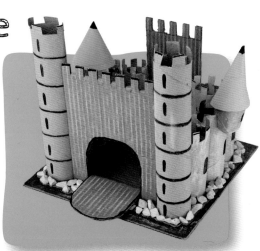

Fun with Paper Plates and Cups!

View from a Lighthouse
32

Busy Bees
36

Stegosaurus on a Plate
38

Predict the Weather
42

Cuptastic Pets
46

You will need a grown-up to help you make these fantastic models.

Get Creative with Boxes!

Monster Eating Money Bank
52

Recycled Robot Mechanic
56

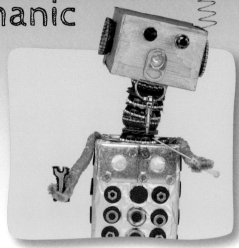

Woodland Theater
60

Decorative Bird Box Light
64

Car Lot Mania
68

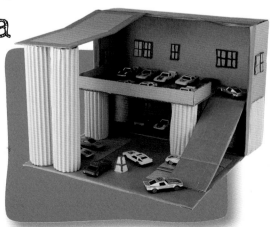

Great Makes with Egg Cartons!

Penguin Island
72

Happy Hens
76

Monsters & Mummies Tic-Tac-Toe
80

Amphibian Friend
84

Ahoy Fish Mates!
88

Useful Items
92

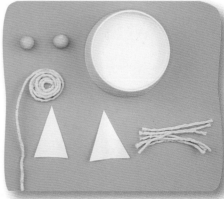

Ready to have fun...

Recycling unwanted things into art is great fun, and it doesn't cost a fortune—all the main ingredients were heading for the bin!

Rescue paper rolls, boxes and egg cartons from your recycling and keep leftover party plates and cups. Use them and get into art. You will soon have your very own art gallery.

You will need...

Materials used
Paper rolls
Paper plates & cups
Egg cartons
Tracing paper
Glue
Pipe cleaners
Cardboard & cardstock
Plastic eyes, beads, or
    buttons
Cupcake liners
Tissue paper
Paper towel
(absorbent)
Cotton balls
Cotton swabs
String
Masking tape
Ruler
Aluminum foil
Bottle caps
Metal pieces
Craft sticks
Milk carton
Cork

Decoration
Paint brushes
Glue brush
Acrylic paints
Pencils
Felt tip pens
Fine line pen
Paper clay
Paper-mache powder
    or tissue soaked
    in PVA glue
Hole punch
Sponge

See page 92 for more information about materials.

Spooky Mates

This spooky centerpiece would be perfect if you ever throw a Halloween party!

You will need...

Cardboard base

Paper rolls x 3

Pipe cleaner (for the cat)

String

Egg carton & tissue paper (cauldron)

Paper (witch's hat)

Paper clay (eyes)

Paint

Glue

Pencil

Spooky Mates

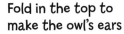

Leave to dry and glue on the hair

1 Trim and paint strands of string a nice bright orange.

Use one paper roll for the witch; paint the body black and the head green.

Paint the mouth and crooked teeth!

Fold in the top to make the owl's ears

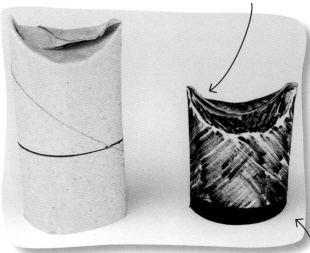

2 Trim a paper roll to make a small owl.

Color or paint the owl like this

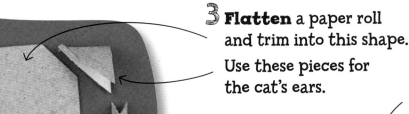

3 Flatten a paper roll and trim into this shape.

Use these pieces for the cat's ears.

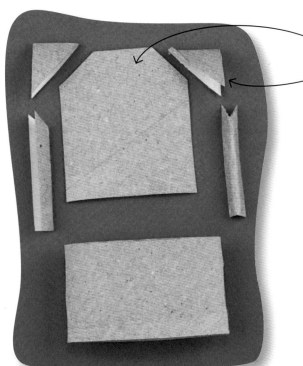

Glue the ears onto the top as shown

To make a curly tail, wind a pipe cleaner around a pencil. Attach it with masking tape

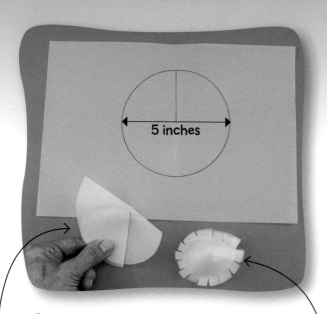

5 inches

5 Make some spooky accessories . . .

Make a cauldron from an egg carton. Add string for a handle.

Build a fire using string. Paint it black and red.

Make a broomstick from a small stick and string, using tape

Use small pieces of paper clay to make eyes

4 Draw around a round object and cut out the paper circle for the witch's hat.

Fold it in half and draw a line to the center, then cut along the line.

Fold into a cone shape and glue into place

Bend to make an edge, cut the rim, and paint it black

6 Paint a cardboard base and all three of the spooky friends.

Give the cat some string whiskers

Paint the cat, then glue on the paper clay eyes

Fill the cauldron with tissue

Zoo Animals

You can make all sorts of animals using paper rolls. These two are real winners!

You will need...

Giraffe
Paper rolls x 4
Cotton swabs x 2
Masking tape
Glue
String
Beads (for eyes)
Pipe cleaner (for tail)
Pens or paint

Zebra
Paper rolls x 4
Pipe cleaner
String
Glue
Plastic eyes
Pens or paint

Recycled animal friends, perfect together!

Zoo Animals
Giraffe

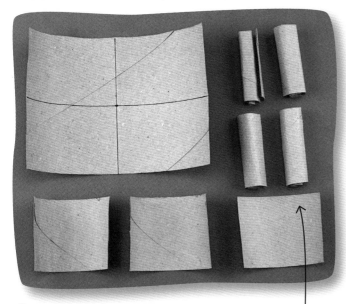

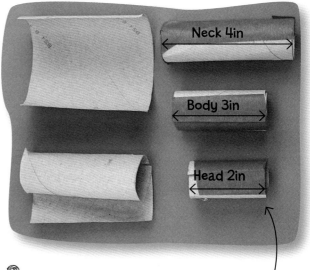

1 **Flatten** a paper roll. Cut down one side, lengthways, and open it out.

Divide into four equal pieces and roll each into this shape to form the legs. Stick together with masking tape

2 **Cut** three more paper rolls lengthways and use them to make the neck, head, and body.

Trim into the lengths shown above and roll into shape.

Neck 4in

Body 3in

Head 2in

Stick together with masking tape

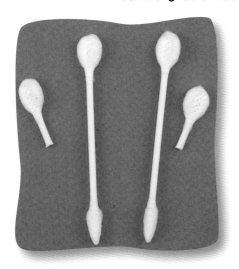

3 **Trim** the cotton swabs and paint them to look like ears.

4 **Make a tail** using a pipe cleaner and string.

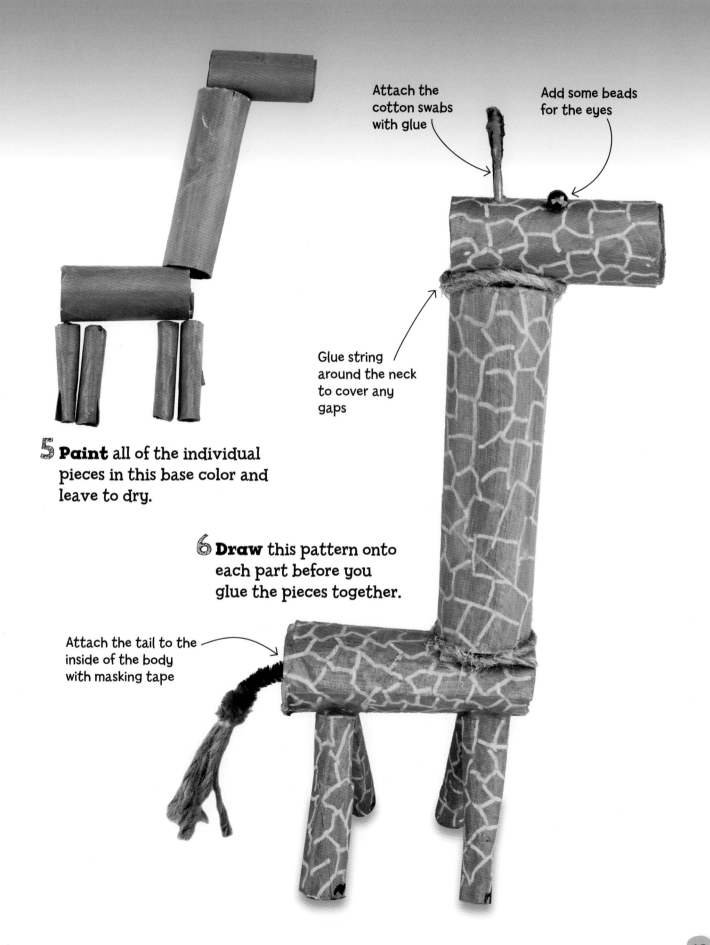

Attach the cotton swabs with glue

Add some beads for the eyes

Glue string around the neck to cover any gaps

5 **Paint** all of the individual pieces in this base color and leave to dry.

6 **Draw** this pattern onto each part before you glue the pieces together.

Attach the tail to the inside of the body with masking tape

Zoo Animals Zebra

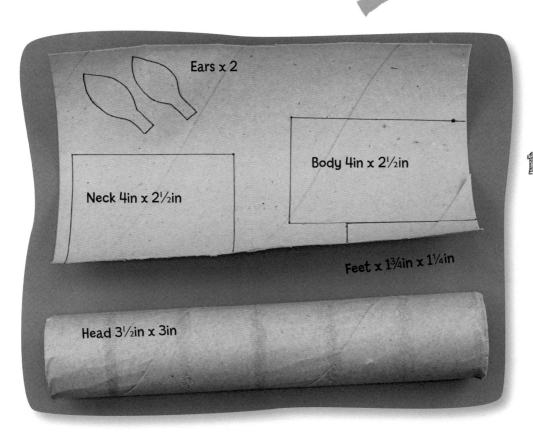

Ears x 2

Neck 4in x 2½in

Body 4in x 2½in

Feet x 1¾in x 1¼in

Head 3½in x 3in

1 **Cut** two large paper rolls lengthways and open them out. Use them to make the body parts.

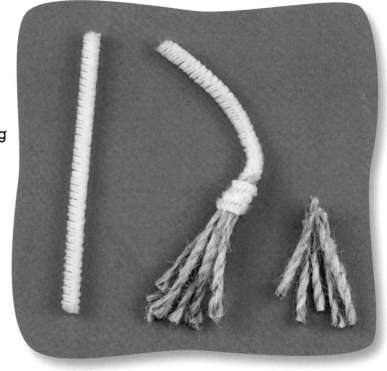

2 **Make a tail** using string and a pipe cleaner.

3 Roll the body into a tube shape and secure the ends with tape.

Then fold the feet in half and stick together with masking tape.

Roll the body into a tube

Fold the head over the top of the neck

Roll the neck into a tube and attach with tape

Fold the feet in half

4 Before you glue the zebra together, **paint** each body part a base color of white. Leave to dry before painting on the black stripes.

Add some big ears

Add large plastic eyes

Don't forget to paint the tail!

Fix the tail inside the body with masking tape

5 Now you can **glue** the zebra together.

Hungry Frog

A game of skill, hold your frog, flip up the fly in one upward arm movement and be ready to catch it.

You will need...

Paper roll x 2
String
Glue
Paper (for template)
Hole punch
Masking tape

Catch the fly in Hungry Frog's mouth!

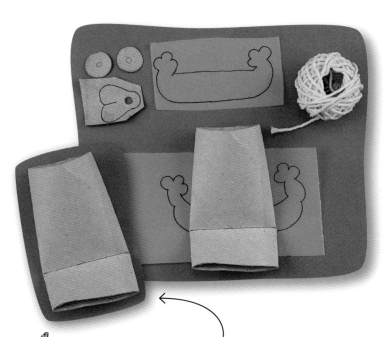

1 Fold the bottom portion of a paper roll like this.

Make a template on paper of the four legs and cut them out.

2 Flatten and cut another paper roll lengthways and open it out.

Glue on the back and front legs and cut them out.

Draw a fly, cut it out and use a hole punch to make a hole

Draw some big eyes and cut them out

Cut a length of string, and make some knots like this

Thread the fly onto the string. Make a big knot at the end so he doesn't escape!

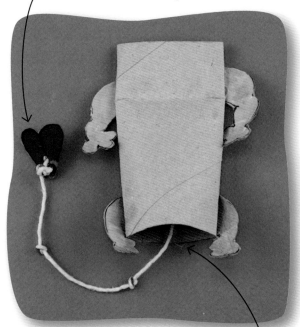

3 Glue the front and back legs to the paper roll.

Attach the string with masking tape and glue.

Glue on great big eyes

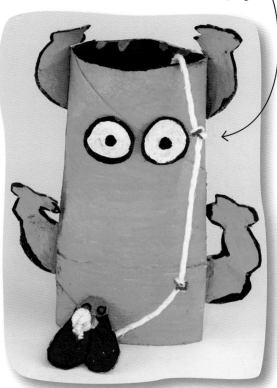

4 Paint the inside red.

Paint the outside bright green.

Crafty Caterpillar

This crafty caterpillar is really useful... he can carry lots of useful things for all your arty projects.

You will need...

Paper rolls x 5
Pipe cleaner
Egg carton
Paper clay (for eyes)
Glue
Paper plate base
String
Pen/pencil
Green paint
Decorations (leaves, buttons, beads, etc.)

This really is a useful caterpillar!

Crafty Caterpillar

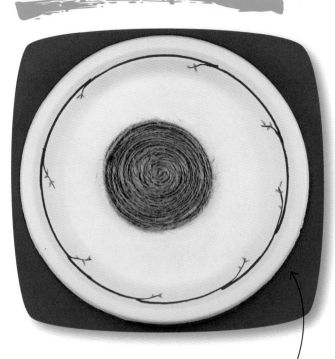

1 **Decorate** the center of your plate with a wheel of string.

Wind the string around and around and glue as you go!

Decorate the edges with paints or felt tip pens

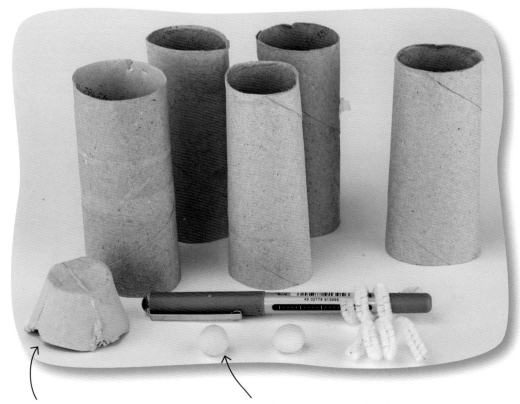

2 **Make** the caterpillar antennae by winding a pipe cleaner around a pen/pencil.

Cut out one of the egg carton cups to make the head

Make some eyes out of paper clay

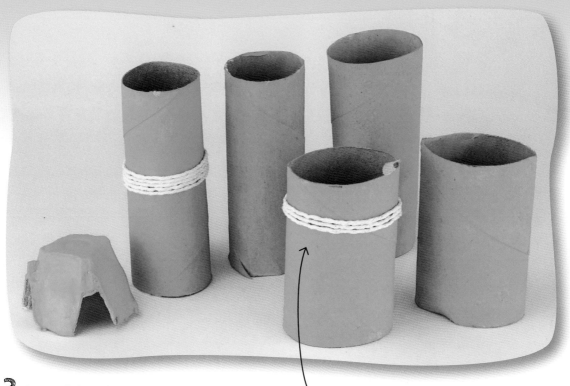

3 Paint the head and paper rolls and leave to dry.

Add some string for decoration

4 Assemble the caterpillar and glue to the plate.

Add a little glue to the string so the paper rolls stick to each other.

Glue on the eyes and antennae

Add your own decoration—leaves, buttons, or beads

Castle

You can make this castle any size you like as long as you have saved enough paper rolls from the recycling bin!

A castle fit for a king and a princess or two . . . and ready for battle!

You will need...

Cardboard base

Paper rolls (large & small)

Corrugated cardboard (for main & rear gates)

Colored cardstock (turret roof)

Glue

Paint

Gravel

Chalk

Castle

1 **Draw** these shapes onto cardboard to make the entrances to the castle.

Cut out the entrance door and the top detail as shown.

Drag the side of a piece of chalk down each piece of the cardboard. Use two different colors

Cut some slits in the top like this

Bend one piece inward and glue it inside, leave the next piece upright

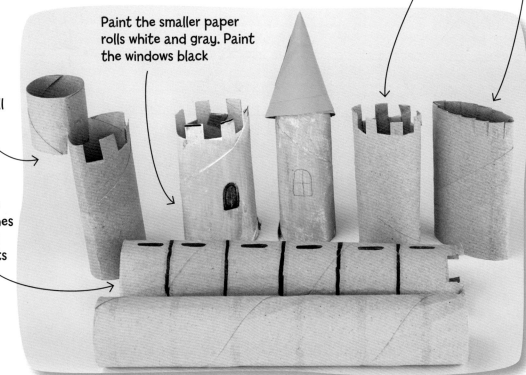

Paint the smaller paper rolls white and gray. Paint the windows black

To make a castle turret, cut a slit and attach to another paper roll

Use large paper rolls to guard the entrance: draw lines around them and draw on arrow slits

2 **Use** small and large paper rolls for the castle walls and battlements.

Use your chalk to color the large paper roll towers.

Draw a line to the centre, then cut along the line

Fold into a cone shape and glue into place

3 Use colored cardstock to make roofs for the turrets. First, draw around a round object and cut out a circle.

4 Assemble your castle on a cardboard base. Choose where you want to put the different pieces.

Leave room for a moat.

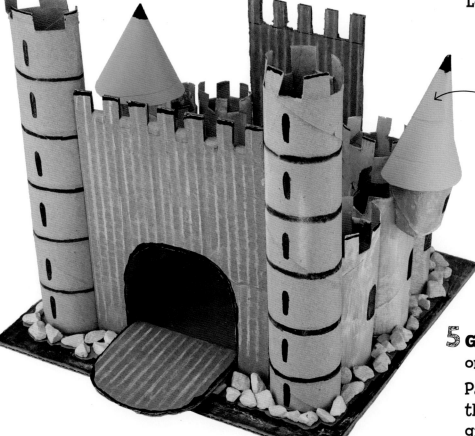

Add a roof to each castle turret

5 Glue all the pieces onto the base.

Paint a moat all around the castle and glue gravel around the base.

View from a Lighthouse

Imagine how fun it would be to look out of a lighthouse window.

You will need...

Tracing paper
Paper plate
Cardstock
Glue
Acrylic paints
Pencil
Felt tip pens
Paint brushes

Make your very own sea view!

View from a Lighthouse

1 **Draw** a scene like this, in pencil, onto tracing paper.

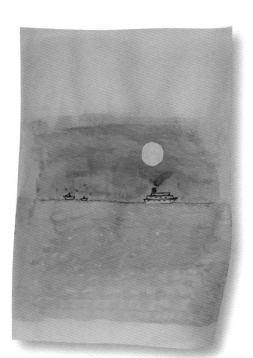

2 **Paint** the sea, sky, and boats. Draw a bright yellow sun on cardstock, and glue it on.

3 **Ask an adult** to cut out the center section of a paper plate.

4 **Draw** some cartoon sea birds onto cardstock. Color them in and cut them out.

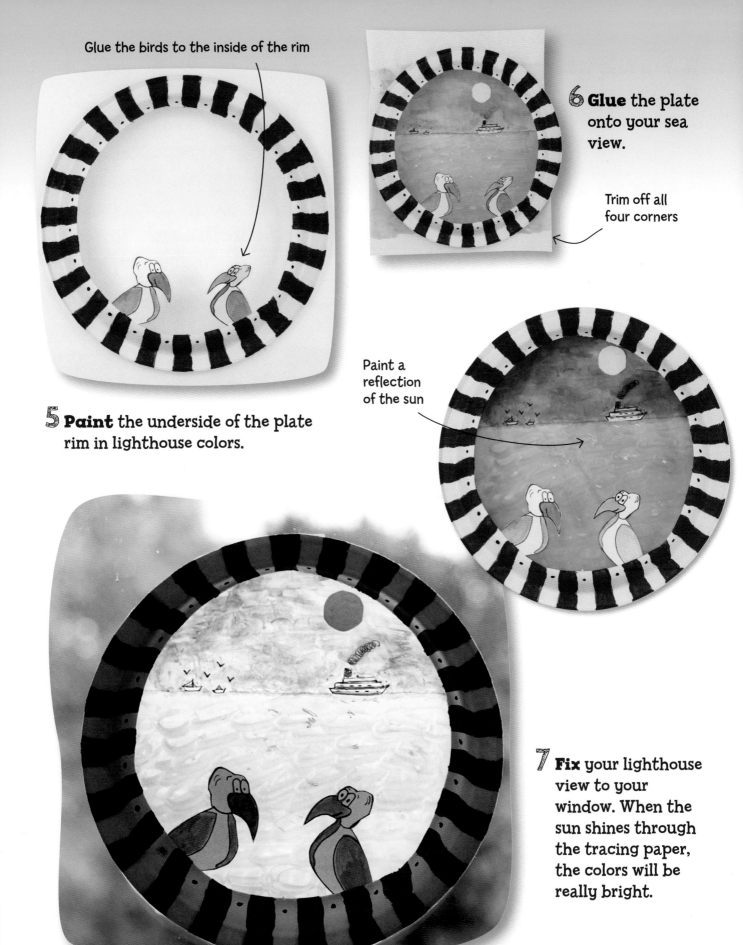

Glue the birds to the inside of the rim

6 Glue the plate onto your sea view.

Trim off all four corners

5 Paint the underside of the plate rim in lighthouse colors.

Paint a reflection of the sun

7 Fix your lighthouse view to your window. When the sun shines through the tracing paper, the colors will be really bright.

35

Busy Bees

Bees are very important friends of nature. Why not make some of your own buzzy bumble bees?

You will need...

Paper cup

String

Stiff cardstock

Floral wire or pipe cleaners

Masking tape

Glue

Acrylic paints

Felt tip pens

Paint brushes

1 **Paint** your paper cup bright yellow. This will be the bees' hive.

When dry, draw on the entrance.

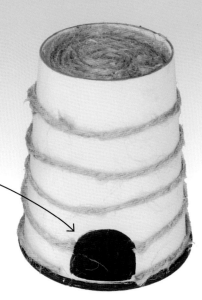

2 **Glue** string in a spiral onto the top of the cup.

Then, glue string around the sides.

Draw this simple shape

Paint the bee yellow

Add some stripes.
Fold the bee in half like this

3 **Make** some bees out of stiff cardstock. Then paint them.

Paint the bees underneath to cover the tape

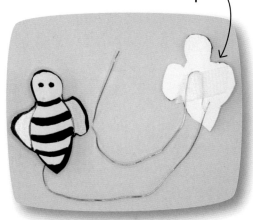

4 **Fix** wire or pipe cleaners to some of your bees with masking tape.

5 **Attach** the wired bees to the hive. Glue on the other bees, too.

Place your beehive by a window. Stick it to a surface with tape. Your bees will fly in a breeze.

Stegosaurus on a Plate!

Stegosaurus is one of the most famous dinosaurs. Why not make your own!

Now he is ready to roar...

You will need...

Paper plates x 3

Corks x 4

Tissue paper

Glue

Plastic eyes or
  paper clay

Glue brush

Clothespin

Stegosaurus on a Plate!

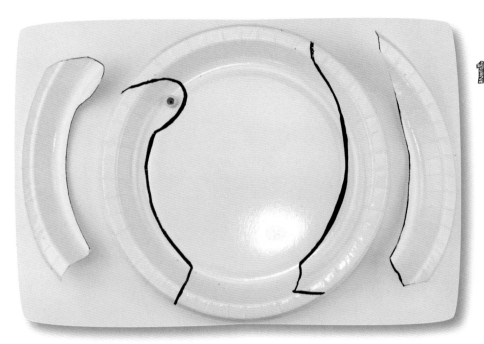

1 Draw the shapes of the head and tail onto a plate and cut them out.

2 Draw triangles on the middle of a plate. Then cut them out.

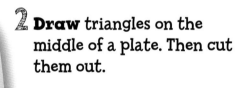

Glue triangles to tissue paper

Cover with another layer of tissue paper

3 Cover four corks in tissue paper for the legs and glue together in pairs.

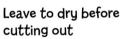

Leave to dry before cutting out

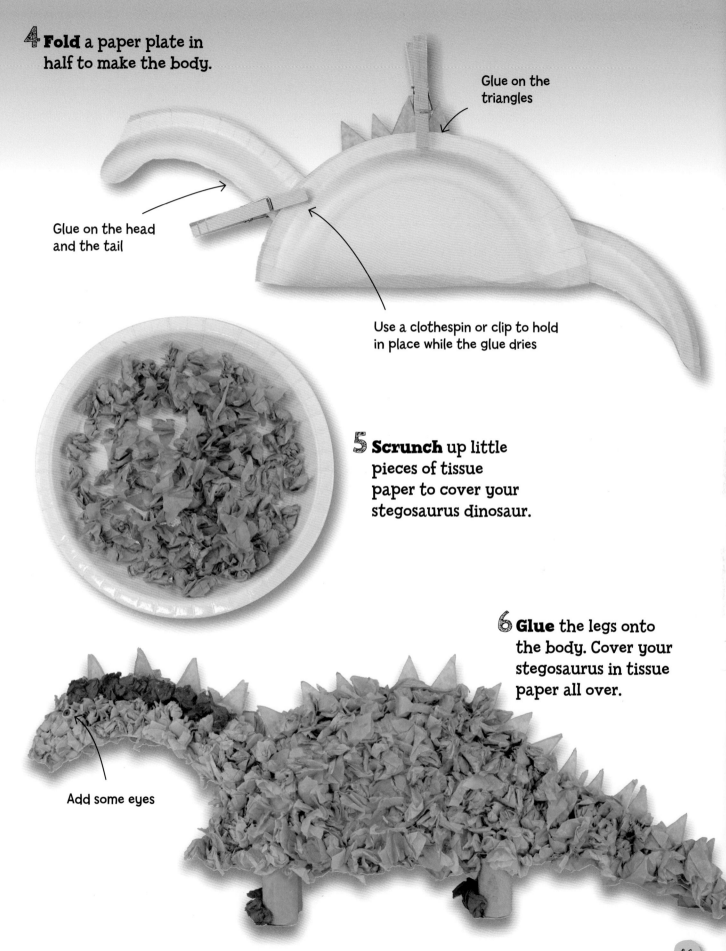

4 **Fold** a paper plate in half to make the body.

Glue on the triangles

Glue on the head and the tail

Use a clothespin or clip to hold in place while the glue dries

5 **Scrunch** up little pieces of tissue paper to cover your stegosaurus dinosaur.

6 **Glue** the legs onto the body. Cover your stegosaurus in tissue paper all over.

Add some eyes

Predict the Weather

Make your own weather chart to predict whether it will be sunny, rainy, windy, or snowy.

You will need...

Paper plate
Cardstock
Pipe cleaner
Glue
Masking tape
Felt tip pens
Paper clay (optional)

How good are you at predicting the weather?

42

Predict the Weather

1 **Turn** the paper plate upside down and mark out six similar sized segments.

Decorate the outside of the plate in bright colors.

Windy

Cloudy

Sunny

Rainy

Foggy

Snowy

2 **Think** of pictures that remind you of different types of weather.

Draw and cut out your own symbols onto cardstock.

Paper clay can be used for the eyes.

3 **Ask** an adult to make a hole in the middle of the plate.

4 **Glue** the weather pictures to each section.

5 **Thread** the pipe cleaner through the hole. Secure it to the back with tape.

Make an arrow and glue it to the pipe cleaner.

Point the arrow before you go to sleep. When you wake up, check to see if you got it right!

Cuptastic Pets

Make these popular household pets out of paper cups and whatever else you have to hand!

You will need...

Paper cups x 4
String
Buttons
Paper clay
Cardstock
Cotton balls
Pipe cleaner
Glue
Acrylic paint
Felt tip pens
Paint brushes

These two really are
the perfect pets!

The cat

1 **Cut** the cat's head and tail out of a paper cup.

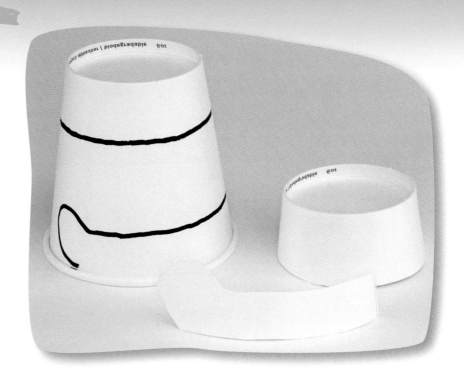

Twist some string like this for the face

Make some eyes out of paper clay

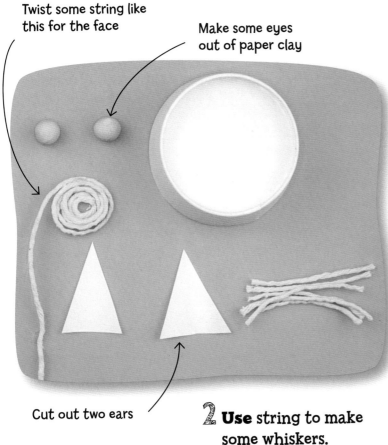

Cut out two ears

2 **Use** string to make some whiskers.

Make some tiny toes out of paper clay

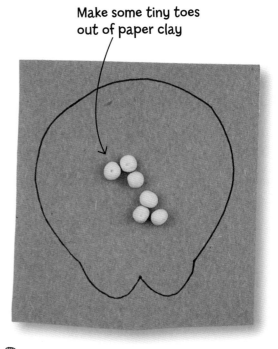

3 **Trim** the top of a second paper cup for the body. On a piece of cardstock, draw around the bottom of the body and add two rounded feet.

Paint a collar at the top

Glue on the tail and add a cotton ball

Glue on the ears, face, painted eyes, and whiskers

Draw on the mouth and nose

4 Paint the head, body, toes, and tail, then leave to dry. Glue the body to the cat's feet. Then, glue on the painted toes.

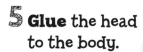

5 Glue the head to the body.

The dog

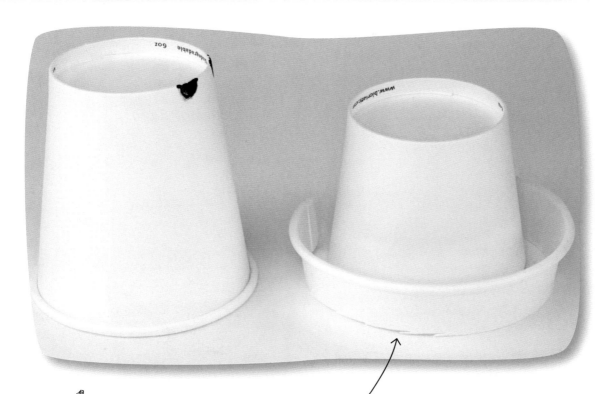

1 **You will need** one paper cup for the body.

Trim another paper cup at the top to make the head and droopy ears.

2 **Paint** a collar onto an upturned cup.

50

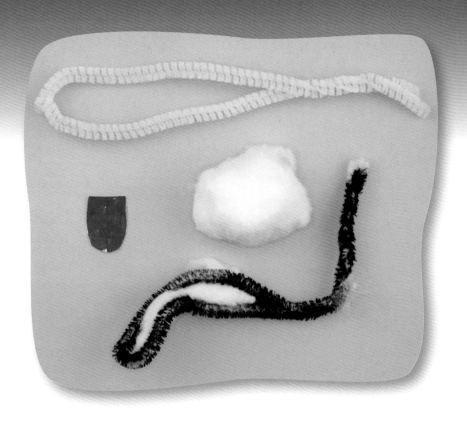

3 **Make** a tail using a pipe cleaner and a cotton ball.

Make a bright red tongue out of cardstock.

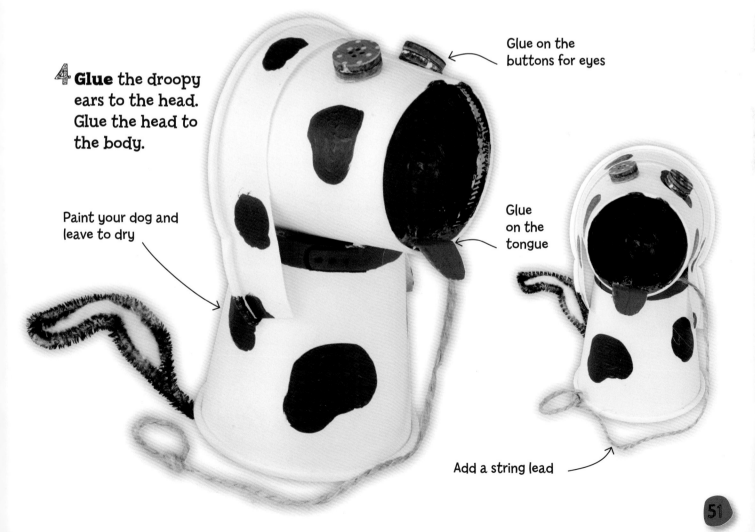

4 **Glue** the droopy ears to the head. Glue the head to the body.

Glue on the buttons for eyes

Paint your dog and leave to dry

Glue on the tongue

Add a string lead

Monster Eating Money Bank

This friendly, hairy money monster looks hungry, but it's a perfect place to hide your hard-earned cash.

You will need...

Tissue box

Cardstock (for teeth and tongue)

Cardboard (eyes and hands)

Egg carton (eyes)

String

Pipe cleaners (arms)

Glue

Sponge

Paints

Masking tape

You are ready to become a monster saving success!

Monster Eating Money Bank

1 **Remove** the opening flap from the tissue box and draw around the shape onto cardstock.

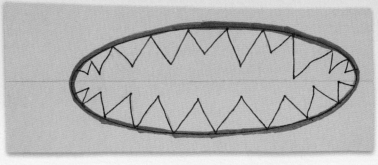

2 **Draw** some teeth.

Cut your drawing in half, then cut out the top and bottom sets of teeth.

Leave space here for some glue

3 **Glue** the teeth to the inside of the box.

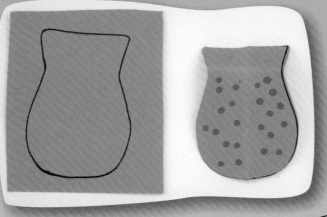

4 Make a monster tongue from cardstock.

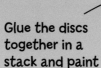

Glue the discs together in a stack and paint

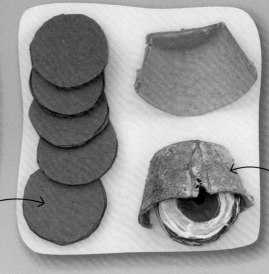

Glue the eyes to the egg carton eyelids

5 Cut out one cup from the bottom of an egg carton, and cut it in half to make two monster eyelids. Cut out 10 discs from cardboard, five for each eye.

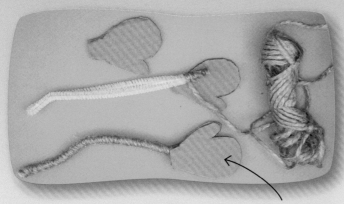

6 For the monster arms, **wind** string around two pipe cleaners. Cut out four hands.

Sandwich one end of the pipe cleaners between two hands and glue together

7 Paint your box. A sponge dabbed in paint works well.

Add some monster string hair

8 Glue on the eyes, tongue, and arms.

Recycled Robot Mechanic

This is a great project for a rainy day. You can style your robot exactly how you want it.

This little robot is a very smart mechanic!

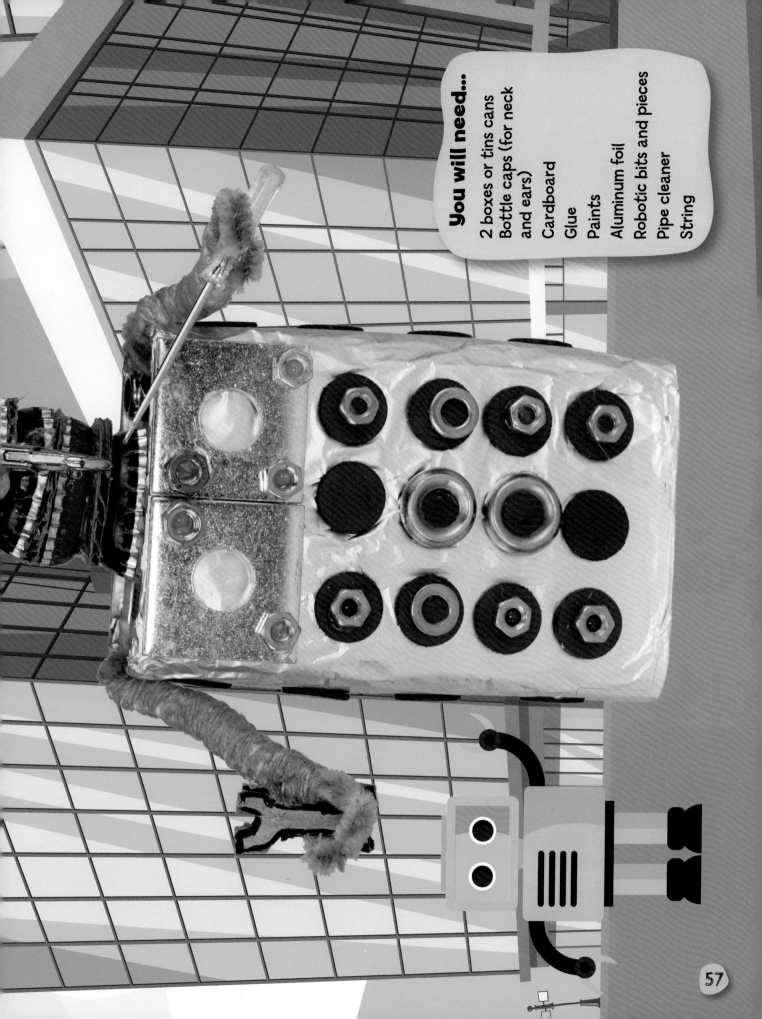

You will need...

2 boxes or tins cans
Bottle caps (for neck and ears)
Cardboard
Glue
Paints
Aluminum foil
Robotic bits and pieces
Pipe cleaner
String

Recycled Robot Mechanic

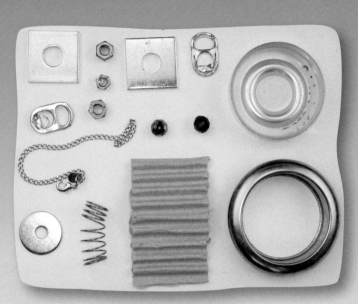

1 **Search** out your odds and ends drawer for robotic bits and pieces.

2 **Cut out** some discs from cardboard. They should be about the same size as your bottle caps.

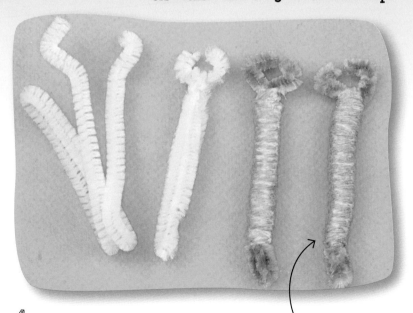

Wind string around, then paint

3 To **make** the robot's neck, glue the bottle caps and discs together in a stack.

4 **Make** some robot arms: fold a pipe cleaner in half and make some pincer claws.

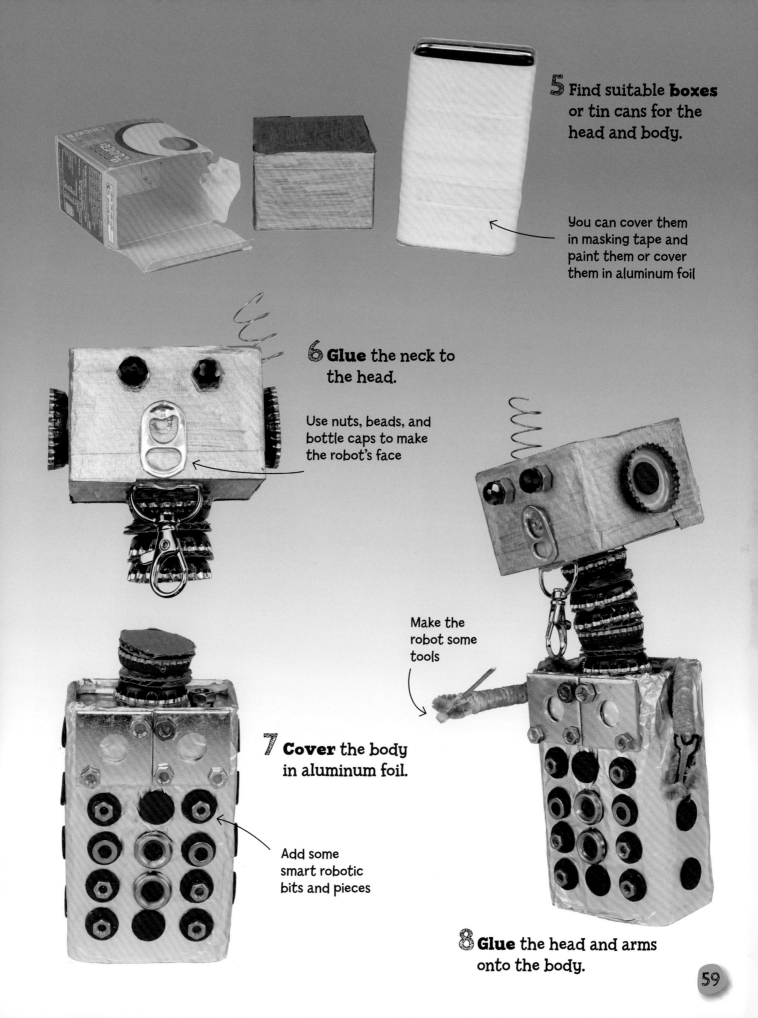

5 Find suitable **boxes** or tin cans for the head and body.

You can cover them in masking tape and paint them or cover them in aluminum foil

6 Glue the neck to the head.

Use nuts, beads, and bottle caps to make the robot's face

Make the robot some tools

7 Cover the body in aluminum foil.

Add some smart robotic bits and pieces

8 Glue the head and arms onto the body.

59

Woodland Theater

You could use fairy string lights for special effects. Good luck with the performance!

58

Create your very own theater and perform plays starring the woodland creatures you make.

You will need...

Box lid or box
Bamboo skewer (optional)
Cardstock
Craft sticks
Beads and painted twigs
Tissue paper
Masking tape
Glue
Paints
Pipe cleaners
Cotton balls

Woodland Theater

1 Ask an adult to **cut out** the middle of the box lid and the bottom portion as shown, and make holes on either side for the skewer.

If your box is shiny, cover it in masking tape so that you can paint it

2 **Draw** a scene on a piece of cardstock and cut it out.

Add some painted twigs for decoration

Use tissue paper for the curtains

3 **Paint** the outside of your box.

Glue the scenery to the inside

4 Decide which characters you would like to star in the show. **Draw** them onto cardstock, color them in, and cut them out.

A bit of a cotton ball makes a great fluffy tail

Add some beads to make the eyes stand out

5 **Glue** them onto craft sticks.

Use a pipe cleaner for a curly tail

Draw feet onto the craft stick

6 Position the theater on the edge of a table (as shown below) and **start the show!**

Use a piece of masking tape to hold it in place during the show

Decorative Bird Box Light

This is a simple thing to make at Christmas time. Add it to your decorations... it's recycling at its best!

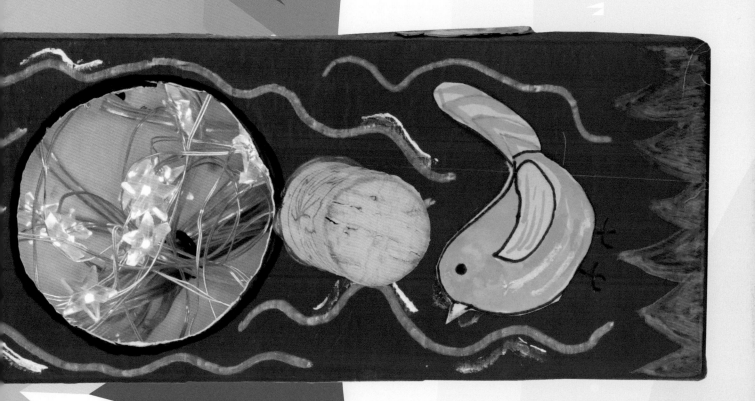

You will need...

Milk carton
Masking tape
Cork
Cardstock
Cardboard
String
Glue
Paints
Battery-operated fairy string lights (optional)

Make your own little piece of Christmas art

Decorative Bird Box Light

1 **Clean** the milk carton thoroughly, and ask an adult to remove the spout.

Cover the waxy surface in masking tape, ready to paint.

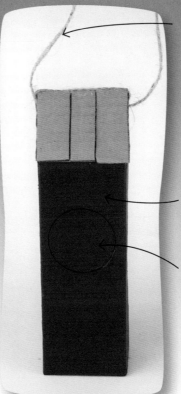

Thread a length of string under the roof if you want to hang the bird box

Paint the background a nice bright color

Ask an adult to cut a hole in the front section of the carton

2 **Cut** small lengths of cardboard for the roof, then glue them on.

3 **Draw** some decorative birds onto cardstock, ready to glue on (it's easier than drawing them directly onto the carton).

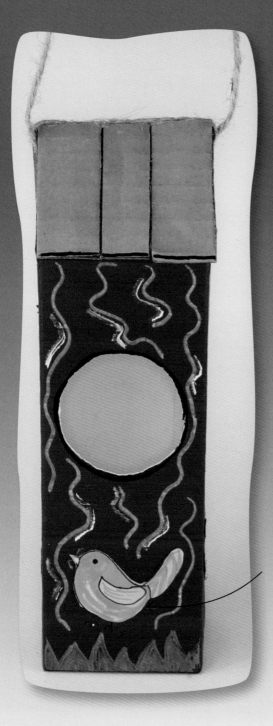

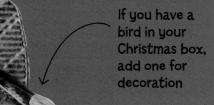

If you have a bird in your Christmas box, add one for decoration

4 Finish **decorating** the bird box.

Glue the birds into place

Add some fairy string lights if you have them

5 A cork **glued** under the hole makes a nice perch.

Car Lot Mania

Car enthusiasts will love building this car lot. It can be up and running in no time at all, and you don't even need paint!

You will need...

cardboard boxes x 2

Colored masking tape

Paper rolls (large x 2 and small x 5)

Egg carton

Corrugated cardboard (optional)

Glue

Felt tip pen

Ruler

Bring in the cars:
parking is free and there
is plenty of room

Car Lot Mania

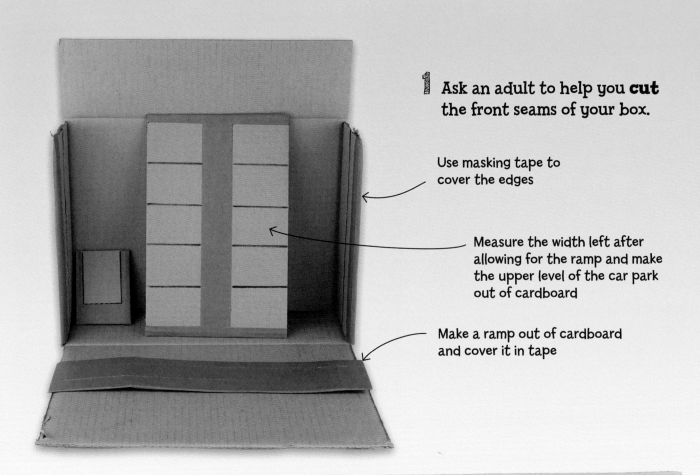

1 Ask an adult to help you **cut** the front seams of your box.

Use masking tape to cover the edges

Measure the width left after allowing for the ramp and make the upper level of the car park out of cardboard

Make a ramp out of cardboard and cover it in tape

2 **Cover** the paper rolls in corrugated cardboard (if you have it).

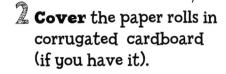

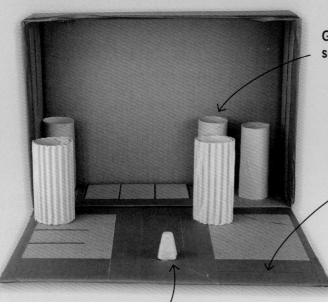

Glue on the small paper rolls to support the upper level

3 Decide on your layout.

Stick down masking tape for the road and use a ruler and felt tip pen to mark out parking spaces.

Add a safety barrier

Make a traffic cone from part of an egg carton

4 Glue the ramp and second level into place on top of the paper rolls.

Glue on the large paper rolls and make an outside roof to fit. Cover the edges with tape.

5 Make some windows for the garage.

Penguin Island

Egg cartons make perfect penguins. Have some fun and make them in all shapes and sizes!

You will need...

Egg cartons
Paper roll
Cupcake liners x 2
Pipe cleaner
Cardboard base
Paper-mache powder or tissue soaked in glue

Paper clay
Glue
Acrylic paints
Felt tip pen
Paint brushes
Glue brush

These penguins are ready to party!

Penguin Island

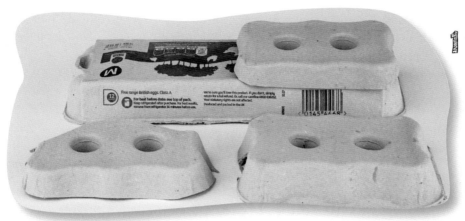

1 **Use the tops** of your egg cartons to make the island.

You can cut them into shapes or leave them as they are.

Leave some areas flat for your penguins to stand on

2 **Paint** a piece of stiff cardboard blue for the sea. Paint your egg carton tops white. Glue your egg cartons into place and add detail with paper-mache or tissue soaked in glue.

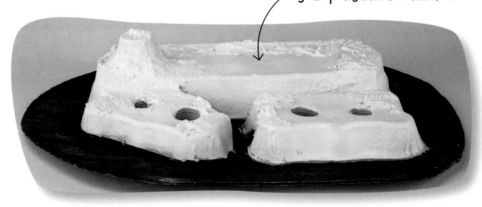

These can be cut to different lengths to make tall or short penguins

3 **Use the bottom** of the egg carton to make the penguins.

Cut the penguins' feet and beaks out of unused pieces of the egg cartons

4 **Paint your penguins** and glue on the feet and beaks. When they are finished they should look like this!

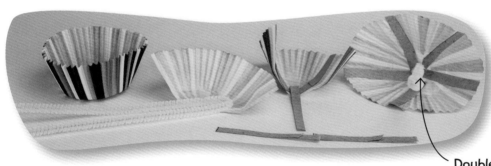

5 To make an **umbrella**, cut a cupcake liner in half.

Make spokes out of cardboard and glue them on as shown.

Glue the two halves together.

Double over a pipe cleaner, wind it around itself, and glue to the canopy

6 **Assemble** all of your penguins.

Add the umbrella

Make a ball from paper clay and use part of another cupcake liner for the towel

Use paper-mache powder or tissue soaked in glue to soften the edges of the island

Happy Hens

These cheeky hens have eyes everywhere and are perfect to keep your eggs safe and sound!

You will need...

Egg carton (size to fit 12 eggs)

Paper clay

Pipe cleaners x 10

Glue

Acrylic paint

Paint brushes

These chilled-out hens look like they are having a good old gossip!

Happy Hens

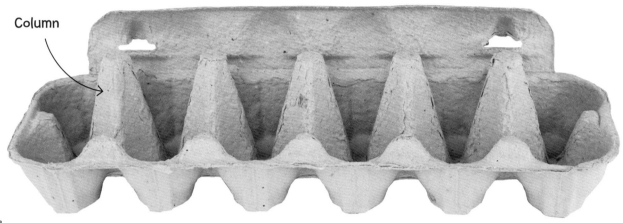

Column

1 **Remove** the top of the egg carton.

2 **Make** ten chicken legs out of pipe cleaners.

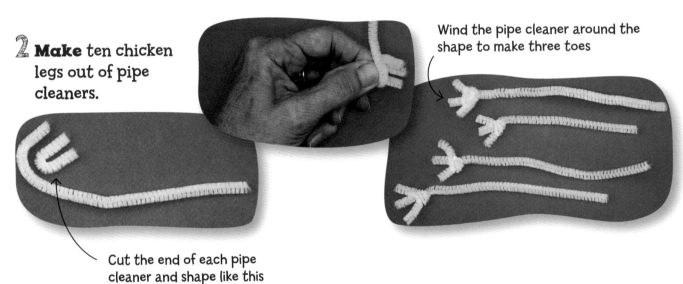

Wind the pipe cleaner around the shape to make three toes

Cut the end of each pipe cleaner and shape like this

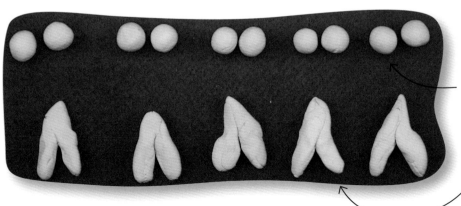

3 **Use paper clay** to make:

Five sets of eyes. Roll small, equal amounts of clay in the palm of your hands

Five sets of wattles, which hang under a chicken's chin!

4 Make five sets of combs for the hens' heads with paper clay.

Bend each comb over the back of a column before the clay dries

5 Paint the legs yellow and the toes red.

Paint the combs and wattles bright red

Paint the eyes yellow

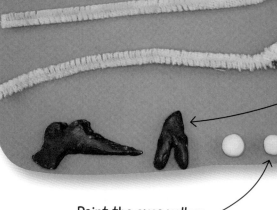

6 Paint the egg carton like this.

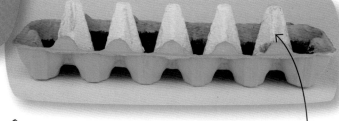

These columns will be the hens. Paint them white

Glue on the red combs and wattles

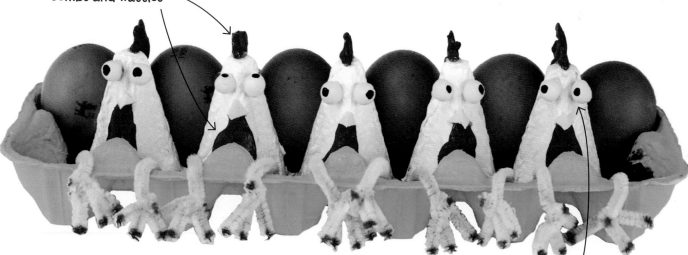

7 Trim the legs so they just hang over the front of the carton. Glue them at the base of the white columns.

Glue on the eyes and draw on the black pupils. Some eyes look left, some right, and some up!

Monsters & Mummies Tic-Tac-Toe

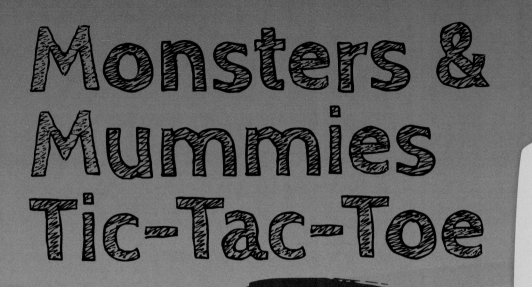

Which is your favorite to win? Choose your side for a seriously spooky game of Tic-Tac-Toe!

See page 92 to see how to play Tic-Tac-Toe

Let the Tic-Tac-Toe spooky tournament begin!

81

Monsters & Mummies Tic-Tac-Toe

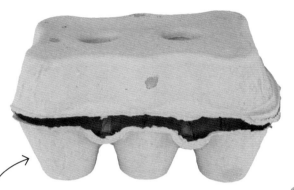

Monsters

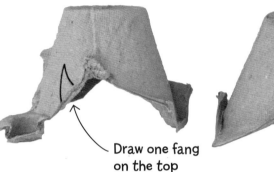

Draw one fang on the top

1 **You need to make** five monsters and five mummies.

Remove the lids of your egg cartons and cut out 20 cups.

2 **You will need** ten of the cups to make five monster. Draw onto the cups as shown.

Add spots and a monster eye

3 The cups go together like this.

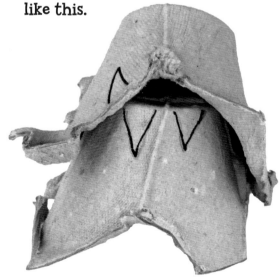

4 **Paint** them a brilliant monster color inside and out.

Glue the monster's head to the body when dry.

82

Mummies

5 **You will need** ten cups to make the mummies! Glue the cups together like this.

Cover in PVA glue afterward. Leave to dry before painting

Add eyes

Leave some pieces hanging for extra spookiness

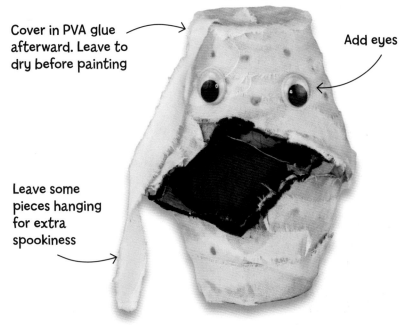

6 **Cover** the surface in PVA glue and wrap all your mummies in thin strips of cotton fabric or paper towel.

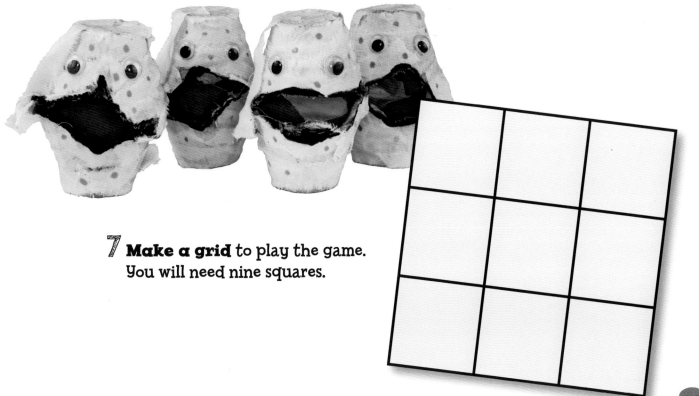

7 **Make a grid** to play the game. You will need nine squares.

Amphibian Friend

This little frog is full of charm and is so cool to make.

You will need...

Egg carton
Pipe cleaners
Glue
Cardstock
Acrylic paint
Felt tip pen
Paint brushes

Everyone will love our boggle-eyed recycled friend.

Amphibian Friend

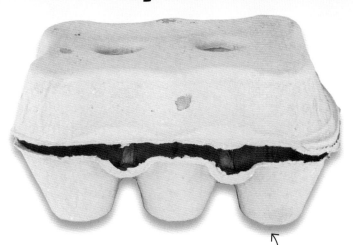

1 **You will need** the top and two cups from the bottom of your egg carton.

2 **Draw** cut lines on the cups like this.

This is the top of the head

3 **Cut them** into these shapes. Paint the inside red and the outside green.

4 **Glue** the frog's head together when the paint is dry.

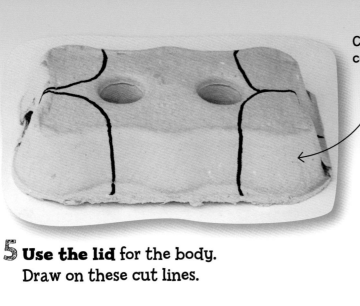

Cut out the four corners of the lid

5 **Use the lid** for the body. Draw on these cut lines.

6 **Glue** the four corners together like this.

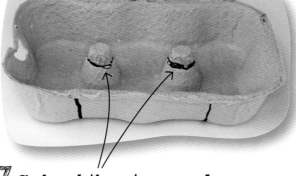

7 **Cut out** these two round discs for the eyes. Glue them together and paint them.

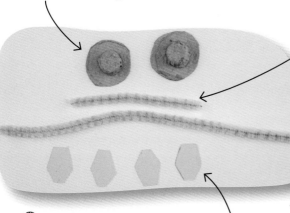

Short legs for the front

8 **Make some legs** from the pipe cleaners.

Cut some feet out of cardstock like this

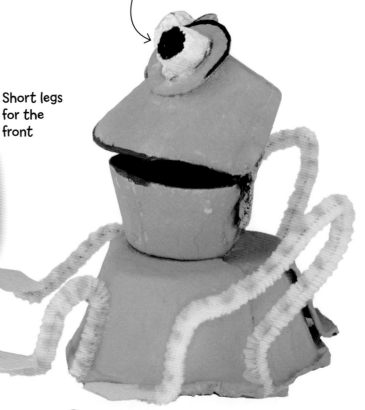

Glue on the eyes and legs, then glue on the feet

9 **Paint** the frog's body green and then glue the head to the body.

Ahoy Fish Mates!

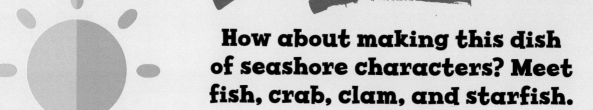

How about making this dish of seashore characters? Meet fish, crab, clam, and starfish.

Assemble your fishy friends—what mischief do you imagine they would get up to?

Ahoy Fish Mates!

Starfish

1 **Use one cup** from the bottom of the egg carton.

Cut triangle shapes like this.

Make some eyes out of paper clay and glue them on

Flatten and glue on a fifth triangle like this

Paint your starfish

Crab

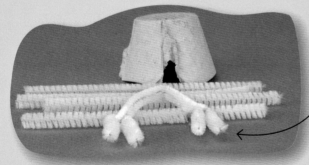

Make some claws from pipe cleaners

2 **Use one cup** for the body.

Cut a pipe cleaner into four short lengths for the legs.

Make some paper clay eyes.

Paint the crab and glue on the eyes

3 **Glue** on the pipe cleaner legs and claws.

Clam

4 Use two cups. Cut them out like this and glue them together.

The mouth is slightly open

5 Paint the clam gray inside and out.

Make some paper clay eyes and glue them on.

Fish

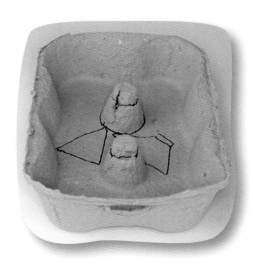

6 Glue together two cups.

7 Use the lid to make...

Fin

Tail

Eyes

Mouth

Cut them out and glue them to the body.

8 Paint your fish and glue to a stone.

Useful Items

Paper clay is great for fine detail. It has been used to make the eyes. Add them to your art box and kids will have hours of fun. You can purchase it cheaply from craft stores and online. A little goes a long way, and it just needs to air-dry before painting.

You can use **plastic eyes** from craft stores or just paint eyes onto the models.

Water jars for cleaning brushes while painting.

One jar for your glue brush

Tissue soaked in PVA glue is a good alternative to paper-mache powder.

Scissors

Ruler

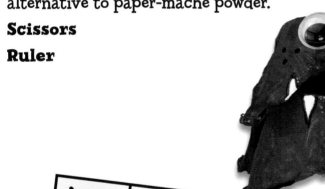

How to Play Tic-Tac-Toe

Draw the board with 3 x 3 squares (9 in total)

Traditionally, each player takes turns drawing a "X" or a "O" on each square. In our game we are using "mummies" and "monsters."

The first player to have a row of the same symbols (or pieces in our game) wins!

Picture Credits

(abbreviations: t = top; b = bottom; m = middle; l = left; r = right; bg = background)

Shutterstock:

First published in Great Britain in 2020 by Hungry Tomato Ltd
F1, Old Bakery Studios,
Malpas Road, Truro,
Cornwall, TR1 1QH, UK

Copyright © 2020 Hungry Tomato Ltd

Beetle Books and Hungry Banana are imprints of Hungry Tomato Ltd

US Edition (Beetle Books)
ISBN 978 1 913077 211

UK Edition (Hungry Tomato)
ISBN 978 1 913077 297

Printed and bound in China

Discover more at
www.mybeetlebookso.com
www.hungrytomato.com